Messages
of
Love
Remembered

*David —
Look at this love
story from
beginning to end —
Amazing!
Best Always,
Stacey*

BOOKS BY MITZI LIBSOHN
"Immortal Kisses – Confessions Of a Poet"
"Songs Of You – A Postscript"
"Silhouettes – Literary Passageways"

BOOKS BY PAULI ROSE LIBSOHN
"What is Love"
"My Mother and Shakespeare – A Daughter's Journey"

Messages
of
Love
Remembered

Pauli Rose Libsohn

Copyright © 2019 Pauli Rose Libsohn
All rights reserved
First Edition

PAGE PUBLISHING, INC.
New York, NY

First originally published by Page Publishing, Inc. 2019

ISBN 978-1-68456-073-8 (Paperback)
ISBN 978-1-68456-074-5 (Digital)

Printed in the United States of America

IN MEMORY OF A TRUE LOVE

This remarkable collection of newly discovered poetic verse

Hidden away in old greeting cards preserved by my mother,

Is in fact, exceptional.

Composed by my parents as expressions of

Love and desire to and of themselves,

These treasured vignettes express their undying devotion,

While revealing the true measure of their endearment

That being – eternal adoration.

Thus, the inception and creation of this collection was born,

Including insights of my parents' personal lives held dear

Documented and written by myself,

Their daughter,

Whom they cherished throughout their lives.

FOREWORD

An approaching July 4th holiday held for me the promise of relaxation. I had been looking forward with great anticipation to sleeping "late" (7:00 a.m.), doing my beloved gardening, and finally tackling a long over-do project – that being the re-visiting of several bags stored on shelves in my basement containing envelopes of papers marked "old bank statements," with the probable possibility of throwing them in the garbage! They had been there for almost twelve years and now I had decided it was time to actually go through them, hopefully eliminating as much as I could. And so, after having had breakfast, and going for a walk, I went downstairs to the lower level of my Condo and into the storage area, headed straight towards those specifically marked four bags packed neatly on their shelves. Determined, I at once whisked them upstairs where I had garbage bags waiting and proceeded to open the several envelopes. What happened next was astonishing! As I began the task of unwrapping each of the rectangular shaped accordion envelopes – a remarkably simple undertaking – it was to my amazement that I found that not only were there no old bank statements to be "unearthed," but that each envelope was stuffed full with old greeting cards that my mother, my father and myself, had exchanged on various ceremonious occasions. Truly, I was swept away by this discovery. "Momentous" would be correct in terms of my reaction. At that instant it became "crystal clear" that my mother had collected and saved these cards with their very personal messages over the years, placing them in these envelopes that had been boldly marked as containing our bank documents that my father had so often drummed into our heads as to their importance, and therefore insisted on us keeping. Now, those bank documents were nowhere to be found! Essentially, I guess my mother felt that these cards and their messages superseded those old statements and took it upon herself to override my father!

Awe and wonderment were sweeping through and around me – I could not get over my discovery. I found myself to be in a state of "stupefication!" After calming down, I began reading each and every one of the greeting cards that my mother, my father, and myself had exchanged over the years, with the realization that the messages of adoration we had so lovingly composed to one another, were exceptional and extraordinary. Cards for anniversaries, birthdays, Father's Day, Mother's Day, Graduation, Thank You, and for "no reason at all," were all included in this collection, with some having dates as far back as the 1940's, along with five extraordinary letters of love. Their beauty, juxtaposed with their depth of emotion, I believe are unequaled in today's world. One would be hard-pressed to find a marriage of today to be equivalent to that of my parents' – the deepest form of love, admiration and respect, with myself included. Therefore, I came to the realization that these messages of love, had to yet again be produced as another publication, as a window in time into my parents' emotions and lives together. I am of the firm belief that the world would have been cheated of this brilliant romantic treatment of a well-worn theme – love – if I had not decided to go forth and once again share it with one and all. And so, I have produced a picture of my parents' emotions rarely seen – allowing their most private feelings and sentiments of the heart to be laid bare, bringing the public into their private world of true love and immeasurable devotion – "Messages Of Love – Remembered."

Pauli Rose Libsohn

CONTENTS

SEPARATION AND REUNION
1. Separation and Reunion 15
2. Darling.. 18
3. My Darling 19
4. My Darling Husband! 20
5. On The Sands Of St. Augustine Beach 21
6. Saturday Night 22
7. Happy 23
8. My Wonderful One... 24
9. Darling!... 25
10. Darling!... 26
11. Remember.. 27

LOVE'S LETTERS LOST AND FOUND
1. Love's Letters Lost and Found 1945 and 1964............. 31
2. August 15, 1945... 35
3. Wednesday 38
4. Thursday, AM 40
5. Monday... 41
6. Monday... 42

HAPPY ANNIVERSARY
1. Happy Anniversary.. 47
2. For David, April 26, 1949 51
3. To Mit –
   The Most Wonderful Wife In The World 52
4. Sweetheart 53
5. Sweetheart 54
6. Happy Anniversary.. 55
7. David Dear 56
8. My Dearest Love 57
9. As Long As A Man… 58

  10. Mit 59
  11. Forever 60
  12. Always 61
  13. Our Anniversary 62
  14. Happy Anniversary 63
  15. With All My Love 64

HAPPY VALENTINE'S DAY – WILL YOU BE MINE?
  1. Happy Valentine's Day – Will You Be Mine? 69
  2. And Your Love 71
  3. Happy Valentine's Day 72
  4. Always in Love 73
  5. …I Love You… 74

MOVING DAY – MARCH, 1971
  1. Moving Day – March, 1971 79
  2. Dearest David 83

MOTHER'S DAY
  1. Mother's Day 87
  2. Measles 89

FATHER'S DAY
  1. Father's Day 93
  2. Love To The Big Fish 97

HEY! HEY! GRADUATION DAY! 1967
  1. Hey! Hey! Graduation Day – 1967 101
  2. Dearest Pauli 103

DAVID'S BIRTHDAYS
  1. David's Birthdays 107
  2. Darling! 111
  3. David Dear 112
  4. Happy Birthday 113

MITZI'S BIRTHDAYS
1. Mitzi's Birthdays 119
2. To My Wife 123
3. Happy Birthday Dearest 124
4. There's Only One You! 125
5. Happy Birthday 126

FOR THE LOVE OF PAULI
1. For The Love of Pauli 131
2. November, 1983 135
3. November, 1985 136
4. November 11, 1988 137
5. November 11, 1991 138
6. November, 1996 139
7. November, 1999 140
8. November, 1999 141
9. November, 1999 142
10. November 11, 2000 143
11. November 11, 2000 144
12. November, 2000 145
13. November, 2001 146
14. Happy Birthday 147
15. November, 2003 148
16. Happy Birthday 149
17. Happy Birthday! 150
18. Dearest Pauli! 151
19. Dearest Pauli! 152
20. Happy Birthday – Dearest Pauli 153
21. Birthday Girl! 154
22. November, 2007 155

A THANK YOU FOR PAULI
1. A Thank You For Pauli 159
2. Dear Pauli 161

A DAUGHTER'S NOTE 163

SEPARATION AND REUNION

"My darling husband – When I could be with him yet on the Long Island Railroad – What a luxury! – June, 1945.

SEPARATION AND REUNION

June, 1945 – The United States Army's "congratulatory" letter that was received by my father in April of 1945, came with the promise that he would be drafted that coming June. And so, when June arrived, that very promise was kept – he was promptly inducted into the Army of the United States. His status as First Class Private Libsohn, came just two months after my parents' miraculous April wedding and their ensuing honeymoon with its fairy tale magic. I can only imagine the moment when their realization came that they would now have to endure a painful separation while my father was at Basic Training in New Jersey's Fort Dix, and then on to an Army Camp in St. Augustine, Florida. It had to be an emotional "wrench" for them both – practically unendurable.

My mother, however, was ingenious! When the day of departure arrived, and it was time for my father to board the special train of the Long Island Railroad, that was to take him to Pennsylvania Station in New York for the first lap of his trip to Fort Dix, New Jersey – his ultimate destination – my mother somehow was able to board that very same train, and travel with my father all the way to Penn Station! In doing so, she recorded the evidence in a cherished photograph that she took of him in that special LIRR car, in his Private's uniform, and in what she composed on the back of that very photo. As demonstrated by her loving hand, her love for her David, was unquestionable!

* * * *

September, 1945, could not have arrived quickly enough for both my mother and my father, for it was to be a cause for celebration – not only because my mother's birthday happened to fall on the 18th of that month, but it was to be the first time since June, after my father's induction into the Army, that they would once again be together! As exhibited by their advanced planning and loving correspondence, there was nothing that could compare with my parents' overwhelming joy as they prepared to be reunited on my father's first "LEAVE." Instructions were given, and reservations were made for my mother's much anticipated trip by train, bringing her to her final destination of St. Augustine, Florida, where my father was stationed. Acting swiftly and with a firm immediacy, my father wasted no time in securing a temporary residence for my mother – it was an unspoken understanding between them – she would live there for the duration of his tour of duty at the Camp, outside of St. Augustine, for neither she nor my father could bear to leave one another – they could not, and would not.

My parents' strong and all-encompassing passion for one another can be realized in several of the many photos taken by them both in St. Augustine. My mother adoringly wrote her many messages of love, composed from the depths of her heart, which appear on their reverse sides. So too, my father was exultant and beside himself with joy, knowing that the love of HIS life, Mitzi, would once again be with him. My father could not exist without HER, nor too, my mother could not exist without HIM – David, the love of HER life! They never forgot St. Augustine, Florida!

Did I ever tell you that I love you?
St. Augustine, September, 1945

DARLING

Darling, we'll never let go –
St. Augustine Beach, September, 1945

And the cars come down to the beach here, and drive
directly along the shore close to the water's edge.

The sand is hard-packed to make a good road,
but it is nonetheless lovely white-clean.

MY DARLING

I'm in China
And I see an enchanted cottage for us very soon
St. Augustine Beach, September, 1945

MY DARLING HUSBAND!

So precious to me today and every day!
St. Augustine Beach, Sept., 1945

ON THE SANDS OF ST. AUGUSTINE BEACH

After a tour of Castillo de San Marcos –
And my husband sent me into the old dungeon first!
Sept., 1945

SATURDAY NIGHT

A Saturday night date with my favorite beau
For dinner at the Castle Warden
And a counting of the stars later
Overlooking the bay in St. Augustine
'neath Florida palms
St. Augustine – "The Town"
Sept. 1945

HAPPY

Happy Happy Day!
With my sweet sweet David
All to myself at St. Augustine Beach!
What joy to be with my husband!
Alone – together!
St. Augustine Beach, Sept. 1945

MY WONDERFUL ONE

My wonderful one
My wonderful wonderful one!
St. Augustine Beach, September, 1945

My darling husband changing the tides from low to high –

DARLING!

You do dance beautifully!
St. Augustine Beach, Sept., 1945

DARLING!

Did you know your wife could dance the shimmy?

REMEMBER

Darling
Remember how lovely
The large full moon over the bay
And we knew it was there
For our sake alone
St. Augustine, Sept. 1945

LOVE'S LETTERS LOST AND FOUND

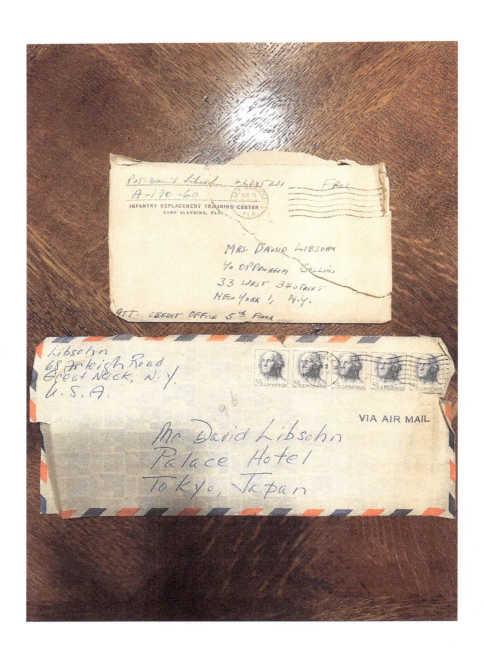

LOVE'S LETTERS LOST AND FOUND
1945 AND 1964

What came as a complete shock and surprise, was the astonishing discovery of a letter written by my father to my mother on VJ Day. I found it to be carefully folded in its original envelope, neatly placed in a beautiful large cranberry and beige flowered container amongst my father's "things," that my mother had neatly packed away. When I realized "WHAT" I had unexpectedly uncovered in the course of my search for old bank statements, I actually had to catch my breath. For once, I was successfully stopped in my tracks, my mind swirling with thoughts, not being able to continue in my "treasure hunt." The significance of this find was tremendous. Over and over again, I imagined how my mother kept this by her side, all these years – it was completely remarkable, but knowing my mother, it was to be expected! She HAD to keep it close. And to think that this letter was never out of her range of "sight," knowing at a moment's notice of its whereabouts, was amazing, for there was never an inkling to me, of its existence. I couldn't help thinking that I kept circling in and around it throughout my life, probably almost coming in contact with it once or twice, under the watchful eye of my mother! I know too, that my father had to know of its existence, just by where it had been stored throughout its "life" of six decades. That letter I realized, went everywhere, with both my mother and father making sure it would be safely tucked away at all times. Once again, I couldn't help but imagine, that on all my parents' various "moving days," that this letter would be upper-most in their minds, again, unbeknownst to me – ever, with them personally transporting it from house to house, drawer to drawer. And, in all those years, they never ONCE told me of its existence, not even alluding to it – the reason being, as I knew deep within my heart, was that that part of their lives belonged to them solely. I had not been part of that segment of their love affair. It was for them only. They considered that to be most precious and sacred. Only after I was born, was I to become part of that love, and not before. I understood. Their passion was so intense and so private, that they could not include me in that aspect of that very passion, about which they were so powerfully protective.

After recovering from the "shock," I carefully read, and reread, over and over, what my father had written, trying to digest it all – a combination of excitement that the war with Japan had ended, detailing what was taking place at the army camp in St. Augustine, Florida where he was stationed, along with his careful and loving instructions to my mother of how to arrange to join him, explaining what type of accommodations she should make for herself, and in turn, that he would make for her. And of course, his endless messages of love!

After having recovered from that surprising event, another was to immediately follow, again, all discovered while I was in search of old bank statements! Caught unaware, I became speechless, when I discovered four deeply emotional and loving letters that my mother had written to my father when he went to Japan in 1964, on a business trip for three weeks' time. I sat very still, again digesting what I had uncovered, running my fingers over the envelopes. Immediately, I said to myself, "Oh my God, my father brought them home." A state of amazement overcame me, when I realized that these precious letters of my mother's, addressed to my father, had come full circle, with their beginnings in Great Neck, New York, sent to Japan, and yes, lovingly brought home with my father. It was hard for me to fathom what I had found, for I vividly remembered my mother sitting at the kitchen table, writing these very letters to my father while he was in Japan, going to the Post Office, sending her precious messages of love to him via AIR MAIL. Never, in my wildest dreams did I ever imagine what a deep emotional divide this had been for my mother, and how she must have struggled to keep up a good appearance, just for me! She again had packed them away, in a large decorative brown and tan envelope. Never would she have discarded them. It would have been unbearable, for her four letters clearly had an extreme emotional effect on my father, which was evidenced by him having purposely saved all four, in turn, packing them up in his suitcase, with the one thought of bringing them back home, to present them as a keepsake of his love, to my mother. It is my belief that they had to have impacted him to such an extent, that he could never part with them, and must have read them over and over, while longing for the sight and touch of my mother.

Finally, all these four letters made me realize once again, of the enormity of the bond that existed between my parents, for it is truly intangible – something that the mind cannot even begin to conceive. The passion and deep emotion with which my mother expressed her intense desire for my father, to the point where she was actually almost unable to function without him, was incredible. However, the way in which she expressed herself in these letters, was one of a Romantic Poet – her feelings surged forth, and lingered on each of her lines. Her love for my father was dramatic, as witnessed by my mother's sensual descriptions of the grand romance existing between them – a dreamlike perfection of love. Her kiss that she leaves for my father at the end of each page, does not disappear into the clouds – it stays forevermore for only him to know, as she bravely professes her profound and subjective feelings of eternal love.

…And we even had a picnic with pears and cookies and candy –
St. Augustine, September, 1945

AUGUST 15, 1945

Dearest Mit –

V-J Day at last – I guess you must have the day off and are going crazy not knowing how to make it pass quick enough – This morning we were lined up on the parade grounds several thousand strong – We then heard a proclamation from our Commanding General – in which he said we should not let up in our training here –

We next went to see the next in the series of films on "Why We Fight." The series is very interesting and educational. Everyone should be made to see them. As yet they are still introductory, showing the many causes of what caused the present World War – The conclusion left was that is was ours first, permitting Japan to occupy Manchuria over the Mukden Incident in 1931 –

Then dearest, we went to another movie in our company area – but what a sickening picture dear – it was on bayonet warfare – I had known that sooner or later we would be taught this subject – but how I hate it as all other subjects connected were only nauseous. We later had an introductory practice instruction in the use of the bayonet – I was the worst pupil of the company –

However dearest, knowing that any such delinquency may hinder my getting a pass when at long last you arrive here, I will rapidly improve –

Darling I love you very much – Don't you care about anybody as I know you don't, but just keep writing as I enjoy your letters to the last scratch. And am grateful I receive two such wonderful letters each day – They really are excellent and I love them knowing that you are right in the end, there –

Mit I shall make arrangements for your accommodations here – however, you have to make train accommodations – and I'd advise you to make them as soon as possible – Dearest – go to Penn Station and make your reservations from there – the main station nearest to camp is Jacksonville – If you can I'd advise your getting a parlor car seat – I think you'd like that better than a Pullman – If you wish get a Pullman – however get a lower berth if possible – I do not know whether you'd like it though, because you do not know who sleeps near you – If you go by Coach – get a pillow from the porter early so that you can sleep comfortably – arrange your schedule so that you do not sleep on the train for more than one night – also take into consideration the fact that the train may be several hours late – you can figure on the trip from Jacksonville to camp at 2 hours – so make all your plans with the foregoing in mind and that I would like to meet you no later than 7:30 PM – You may not be able to make perfect time all around – but if you have to, get here several hours sooner than later – because you can always meet me at the service club at Dix –

PLEASE MAKE THESE TRAIN INQUIRIES AND RESERVATIONS IMMEDIATELY SO THAT YOU GET THE BEST ACCOMMODATIONS – OTHERWISE YOU MAY GET STUCK – Remember, try to get Parlor Car accommodations first – I'll go over all the other details with you as soon as I get the necessary information from you as to what reservations etc., you've made. – however, this Sunday I shall make accommodations for you all the way through to Sept 17 –

Dearest I love you very much and am very glad and happy that we will see each other soon – it is only 4 weeks off and it will be something to look forward to – I do not think there will be any change in my situation – but in case there should be we will make changes accordingly – so please take care of your end immediately.

Dear I've always known you were an unusual and wonderful person – it was only a matter of time before my mother would find out and I'm glad she found out soon – I am glad you were over to see her –

Remember dear – put the money in the bank –

A great big hug and kiss to speed you on your way – and much more when you arrive –

Your most adoring admirer –

David

Together – So happily together!
St. Augustine, Florida, September, 1945

WEDNESDAY

My Dearest Dearest David –

Letting you go last night was one of the most difficult moments we'd had to face up to ever – All my love for you was struggling for articulation and I felt powerless to express it all because how CAN one? A lifetime of love and experience shared so close has left the SELF of us interwoven and your leaving was truly a wrench with pain. The aftermath. All my feelings for you – of the very deepest kind kept coming over me in great waves of emotion all last night, and today I awoke thinking of you and only the sweetness and goodness of you which make me love you so. My involvement with you is so complete and such a total thing that any separation from you is poisonous and fills me with longing for the warmth that flows from you to fill my deepest needs.

I know this trip is so vital and that it fits into everything you have worked so hard for. I am absolutely confident that this trip will broaden your horizons in every way and that it will reinforce our future with Marubeni. I ache with loneliness for you, but you must know that the unemotional side of me is fully aware of all the advantages involved in your connections with Marubeni being carried over with a trip to Japan. Your brilliant qualities and flair for business intrigue can now fully be realized and appreciated. This is the exciting moment for you and with all my love, I want you to strut like a peacock, puff like a pheasant, crow like a rooster, fly like a bird and ring like a bell! Everything has led to this! Be noisy, be strident, and be my love!

Everything has an end result – be strong in the knowledge that I love you so and that you have this to turn to in me, and that you have succeeded in what you are doing. I share in all your optimism, so please relax about everything. Do take care of yourself and get plenty of rest, good food and quietude if you can. How I wish I could be with you for all the new and wondrous experiences you will be having in Japan! But tell me something of them in a letter which I anxiously await and which will calm and soothe me a little bit. I am sure you have made a tremendous impression on your new Japanese friends – I envy their being with you!

Pauli is fine but felt so sad last night – She will write to you separately.

Dearest – all my love goes out to you, and you are constantly in my thoughts. Stay well and I embrace you in this little farewell.

Mitzi

July 1964

THURSDAY, AM

Dearest Dearest To Me!

    Your message for me came by telephone via Jess – And oh how I wished for the sound of YOUR voice not his! I am thrilled to know that all is well, and of course, filled with frustration not knowing your feelings and reactions at this very dramatic moment in your "business career." I have so many questions that want answering – all about the people you are meeting, the opportunities involved, the signs all around you, the food, the accommodations, the COUNTRY! – And how YOU are faring in this new sea around you. I feel sure that you have made a tremendous impression on all who have met you, but I am hungry for daily blow-by-blow descriptions of it all, and I am eager to hear of it from your very own lips. Be like a sponge and soak it all up so that a small part of the glamor (?) excitement (?) and drama (?) will rub off on me – I want so much to share this with you, even if I must settle for it in a second-hand way. When you return home, you will be allowed to do ALL the talking non-stop. Now that I am face-to-face with the fact that you are THERE and I am HERE, I am working very hard at the acceptance of this fact – there is a surge of loneliness and a yearning for the sound of your voice, and there is a void in the hum of things – I long for your return – make it soon! Make it soon! Your days must pass quickly – take care of yourself my sweet and don't experiment with too strange foods and get plenty of rest.

    Local news: I spoke to your mother – all is well and we will call her regularly.

    Pauli is fine and being good. She really misses you so much.

All my love goes out to you always –

Mitzi

MONDAY

Dearest David –

    Today a letter from you in which you FINALLY acknowledge a letter from ME! The sound of your voice as it comes to me through your letter is just what I need – The weekend was SO lonely without you. I love your letters but you haven't told me anything about what you are doing vis-à-vis Marubeni. I know you're busy working – but what are you working at, what have you seen in the factories, and what does it mean in terms of when you get back? What are these factories like, what are they producing and how do you fit in? I feel frustrated not knowing the answers to any of these questions – but somehow I'll have to wait to hear about it all until your return. And that's another thing – what about your RETURN – You haven't mentioned any homecoming date at all – And I'm terribly restless to know when you'll be getting back to OUR civilization. Why haven't you mentioned any homecoming date? I miss you and need your presence to restore my sense of BEING once more. I was hoping you'd be home by the weekend. I feel uninformed not knowing what you're DOING and when to expect you home. Perhaps by the time you receive this letter you will be making preparations to leave Japan. Don't delay coming home – make it soon! Being without you this way is just not BEING.

    Memorial Day weekend has come and gone – Missed you! But it was pleasant at the pool – my thoughts were of you. Pauli is brown and is making her usual noises around the house – She misses you too! And is very busy studying for finals. The weather is cool and rainy now and I wonder how it is where you are – Please know that I love you from the DEEP of me and that I find this separation an irritant now – I want you home to stay! – Home is where I am – waiting for you –

All my love – Mitzi

PS – Pauli sends love and kisses too!

MONDAY

My Dearest Dearest –

 It was so wonderful receiving your letter (of Thursday,) and postcards today. It renewed the feeling of being in touch with you after these many days without the sight or sound of you. In reading what you had to say, I hung on every word and then I relaxed with it and read it over for the sheer excitement and joy of having you all to myself again – even if only this way. I was thrilled to learn that you had a good flight over – Your description of its beauty was quite vivid and it was good to know that you met an old acquaintance with whom you had a great deal in common just by being thrown together out of coincidence on this flight. "Small world."

 Your contact with the people who are your "hosts" is just what I expected – I knew you would receive a warm welcome and that they would be tremendously impressed by you and your talents. I share in the glow of this moment and I feel confident as you do, that this moment is here to stay and that it will influence the security of our future. Somehow, I suppose everything has led to this and now you are at the peak where your techniques have a finish and a fine point, where your power to persuade and to maneuver has achieved a brilliance – And I want you to feel prideful towards yourself and to put wings on your EGO and let it fly around the room and when it comes back to you, nurture it lavishly and let it grow! I love executives with swell heads – especially you whose executive round-the-clock managing I miss so awfully much – I'd give anything to be able to take an order from you now – I wonder what it would be, because I just know that you must have one for me.

 Pauli and I spent a hot weekend together – we had a little heat wave with temperatures up to 92 – 94 degrees on Saturday and Sunday! What a perfect time for the pool to have opened! But no doubt it will rain for the Memorial Day weekend, since we have had no rain at all in a long time. It was too hot for sunbathing, so we just sat around in bathing suits and kept cool with the hoses running. The weekend was lonely without you, and I was thinking about you and hoping you had received our mail to give you a feeling of "home." Although I am resigned to this "mission" of yours to Japan, I miss you SO! – and I feel now that each day brings you closer to me. Pauli misses you too and sends you her special noisy kisses – She can't wait to have you home again and to hear from YOU all about this most exciting trip.

My love, I will close now with my lips on yours, and my arms around you – take care of yourself, for I LOVE YOU SO!

Soon! Soon!

All my love,
Mitzi

Mitzi – Ever Adoring,
July, 1964

HAPPY ANNIVERSARY

Mitzi and David going out on the town!

HAPPY ANNIVERSARY

For as long as I can remember, each year when my parents' anniversary rolled around, there was always an air of "grand anticipation." My father would go "card hunting" for months, in search of one, two, or three perfect greetings to present to my mother, composing new verse to include in each of his choices, appropriate only for her. My father gave great care to this occasion, always purchasing a wondrous gift for my mother, after she inevitably would drop her MANY, and ultimately successful hints!

I recall one such time when there had been a Schiaparelli fur coat that she had been dreaming of – my father of course conceded and agreed to accompany her to see this famous "creation." I of course wanted to go along, and so the three of us went to Saks Fifth Avenue to watch my mother model this beloved coat. Always thinking ahead, my mother had placed the coat on hold, and when it was brought out for her to try on, she was instantly transformed! She knew exactly the reaction it would create, due to her uncanny sense of fashion, for my mother always had that certain flair! I watched my father's face – he "fell in love" in that one singular moment with the elegant and magnificent look of that coat, but most of all in the dramatic change that overcame my mother! There was never a question – he made the purchase – the coat was hers! That fur was exceptional – and was styled in the fashion of a chemise. In addition, it had exceptionally large Dolman sleeves, with the fur pelts being on the diagonal throughout. My father and I had never seen anything so finely crafted and gorgeous. Immediately, alterations were ordered, miraculously being completed by the end of that very day. The three of us went for a celebratory lunch, returning to Saks just before closing, to be presented with my mother's precious new coat. Smiles were pasted on all our faces. My mother "danced" out the store! EXQUISITE. That is the only word I can use to describe that coat, and how my mother looked in it – but most of all she dazzled my father!

Another "grand" celebration, was for my parents' fifteenth wedding anniversary. On one of our many trips to Manhattan, my father bought for my mother a gorgeous white gold filigree ring – I even remember the jewelry store they went to on Fifth Avenue – it was "beyond" elegant – I was so impressed! That anniversary was a big number, and to commemorate those years, my father wanted something very special. I, to this day, remember how thrilled my mother was, especially when my father placed that ring on her finger on top of her original wedding band and looked into her eyes – they were both transfixed – it was as if they were actually being married all over again. My mother looked at him and my father looked at her – they "sealed" the purchase with a kiss! That ring stayed on her finger until the end.

My mother too, went to great lengths in search of the "perfect" card for my father. Additionally, she ultimately would present him with several of her picks, always with a small poem that she would write about their unending love. Further, she would unfailingly find him some gift of clothing that he would always respond with "… oh, I don't need that, why did you get that for me?" And she would reply "…try it on, you need it!" He would always smile, try it on, and realize she was right. However, with each anniversary, both of my parents would, without fail, buy one another a book that they had read about in "The New York Times," presenting them to one another with fanfare of the most impressive kind, never forgetting to inscribe them with their messages of love.

I too, went hunting for extraordinary cards to present to my parents – ALWAYS three in number. It was a mission that I loved, starting months in advance so that I would not be caught without a very special greeting!

In addition, my mother always ordered "her" very special cake for my father, since their anniversary would not have been complete without it – it was the "critical" part of the celebration. My mother would inevitably come home days in advance and go over the choices with me that she had devised. After much discussion, and agonizing over what she thought my father would like, we settled on something we believed to be extraordinary, ordering it from my mother's adored

French bakery. When the day of their special day arrived, my mother made sure she made my father's favorite meal for dinner, followed by that all-important and anticipated CAKE! My father's eyes were glowing. Then, after blowing out the candles that my mother had strategically placed, and making a wish, he always got up from the table, hugged my mother and said "…hey lovey, how did you know?" My mother would respond with "…I just did!"

Yet, when I was very young, my parents always went out to dinner in Manhattan at some fantastic restaurant that my mother had researched, and afterwards, attended a long-awaited Broadway show, for which they had gotten tickets for months in advance! And some years, they would just go out for an evening of dinner and dancing either in Manhattan, or on Long Island. But that all came to an end when they moved to their dream home in Brookville, Long Island. Then, they just wanted to celebrate in the "paradise" they had created, just the two of them and myself, all being together. That's all they ever wanted, along with their famous "messages of love."

Curiously however, there was one anniversary celebration that remains as a wonderful and sweet memory. My mother made a special purchase for herself and my father. She had forever been "in love," with a certain song. She absolutely adored it, and felt it was representational of the love between she and my father. That song was "Friendly Persuasion (Thee I Love)," from the movie of the same name. It was first sung by Pat Boone, and then by of all artists, Aretha Franklin. One day, my mother asked me to go to Record World and place a special order for both recordings – Pat Boone's and Aretha Franklin's. I could understand Pat Boone, but I could not understand my mother and Aretha Franklin. But when I heard Aretha sing that ballad, I immediately understood – it was breathtaking, especially with her trademark powerful voice. And so, when the albums arrived at the store, I picked them up and brought them home. My mother was at the door awaiting my arrival with a certain pent-up excitement. When I walked in she said, "…let me see." She became quite animated, anxious to play them both, immediately having me turn on our stereo, which wafted throughout our home. I was floored by the beauty of the song – and I loved both versions – Pat Boone's was magnificent, but Aretha Franklin's was even more so! I was shocked! The song was intoxicating and the voice was pure rapture! My mother was right!

When the day of my parents' anniversary arrived, my mother made sure she knew when my father would be walking through the door. The song was playing – Aretha's version – my father opened the door and walked in – stunned – my mother said "Well?" And my father said "Lovey, you're the greatest!" My mother played that song forever. My father loved her forever.

Mitzi and David, 1966

FOR DAVID, APRIL 26, 1949

"Since I have set my lips to your full cup, my sweet,
Since I my face between your hands have laid,
Since I have known your soul and all the bloom of it,
And all the perfumie rare…
Since it was given to me to hear one happy while,
The words wherein your heart spoke all its mysteries,
…and since I have seen you smile,
Your lips upon my lips, and your eyes upon my eyes;
…Since I have felt the fall, upon my lifetime's stream,
Of one rose petal plucked from the roses of your days;
I now am hold to say to the swift changing hours,
Pass, pass upon your way, for I grow never old,
One rose that none may pluck, within my heart I hold."
Mitzi

TO MIT —
THE MOST WONDERFUL WIFE IN THE WORLD

I've started and stopped so many a time
To express by words' fancy and in rhyme
Of the JOY and HAPPINESS that's filled my life
Since, five years back we became Man and Wife.
Let's not forget that cherished day
No matter how fast time flies away
For it's brought such a treasure of happiness, dear,
Strengthened so firm to form of our love, an unending Weir.
Your adoring Husband,
David
April 26, 1950

SWEETHEART

Unlike the south wind that winds its way away –

I shall stay, forevermore your kiss to know…

You are more than ever my sole happiness

And heart's desire.

Adoringly,

Mitzi

April 26, 1950

SWEETHEART

The years fly by

To become memories

That hang in the heart like a star –

I live only for the lifetime of beautiful memories

That are yet to be ours.

Let my heart always speak to yours as it does now -

With the deepest most adoring love

As to be blessed –

Ever near, ever dear

Mitzi

April 26, 1951

HAPPY ANNIVERSARY

Feeling like a crown of flowers for this day –
All my love and kisses,
Mitzi
April, 26, 1963

Mitzi, 1963

DAVID DEAR

I saw you one morning

And I knew I would love you

All the day through.

Always near,

Mitzi

April, 1964

MY DEAREST LOVE

The long of it is

That I still have promises to keep –

Always!

For those blue eyes I love so well –

Always!

Always will I stay

And you'll know this is only the beginning –

For us a toast to a

Million tomorrows in your arms –

Mitzi

April, 1967

AS LONG AS A MAN…

As long as a man is
Well-loved by his wife
Why should he need the Love
Of the rest of the world.
Happy Happy Anniversay
Dearest.
With all my love forever and forever.
David
April, 1970

MIT

They say that every man

Needs a dream

And you have been my dream

For over fifty years.

With all my love,

David

April 26, 1995

FOREVER

Forever, Happy Anniversary.
To the most wonderful wife
From her ever- adoring husband
David
April 26, 2001

ALWAYS

In you I have found the
"Ideal Husband"
All my love Always
And still – Always!
Mitzi
April 26, 2001

OUR ANNIVERSARY

You could never be ordinary…
Happy Anniversary
To a most extraordinary
Wife!
With all my Love,
David
April, 2003

HAPPY ANNIVERSARY

You always sweep me off my feet!
Amazingly –
Still in Love!
Mitzi
April, 2003

WITH ALL MY LOVE

As always
With all my love
Happy Anniversary.
Your ever-loving husband
David
April 26, 2003

Merrymaking with my darling husband,
at St. Augustine Beach - 1945

HAPPY VALENTINE'S DAY — WILL YOU BE MINE?

First Valentine's Day Married

HAPPY VALENTINE'S DAY — WILL YOU BE MINE?

Valentine's Day! When the day of February 14th arrived, my parents ALWAYS had a bevy of cards waiting for one another on our kitchen table, to be found the morning of, placed there "secretly" the night before, by both my mother and my father, each tiptoeing in, to leave their messages of love. In addition to their cards, my father always managed to find greatly prized and unusual chocolates for my mother, searching far-and-wide for the "perfect" box of these treasured delicacies, for my mother was a true "chocoholic" in every sense of the word! As long as I can remember, she savored "her" dessert time, for she would always incorporate cherished pieces of these delectable delights at the end of her meal, even though she had her traditional dessert before, "topping off" the entire experience, sating her palette with these precious mouthfuls! And, according to my mother, dessert time, became "any" time at all – in the morning to give her a "boost," in the afternoon, for a quick "pick-me-up," and so on and so forth! My father made sure, on February 14th, to surround her with these nuggets of "desire," making "all" her fantasies come true! In addition to all this "chocolateness," I too was not to be left out of the "mix," for it was inevitable that my parents would also find a scrumptious box of chocolates for me, sending them via Messenger, to me at my place of business, never missing one Valentine's Day! I would unfailingly act surprised, and telephone them with "gobs" of thanks, bringing them home at the end of the day, knowing my mother would be waiting! For it was she who picked out these valued chocolatey squares, with them always without fail, being Marsh Mellows, covered in the thickest and darkest of chocolate! There would be hugs, kisses and of course laughter – she always said, "…you knew they were for me, but you can have one if you wish."

Their cards which were purchased by them for one another, were habitually highly original and unusual, so that there was never a doubt tremendous care and thought were put into this effort. I in turn, also gave them my cards of love, invariably, always more than one, since I was never able to decide, and which they cherished along with theirs. They too would give me a card or two or three and write an original cheery verse, which always brought a broad smile to my face.

On the morning of Valentine's Day, we all delighted in the fun of opening our cards, reading and exchanging, laughing and proclaiming our love! And then, there was always the exchange of my parents' beloved books! My mother presented my father with her choice, with the grandest of fanfare, my father smiling and giving her a big kiss! My father in turn, repeated the process with his choice, and then there were kisses galore! But the best part of that day, was to be in the evening, when my mother would bring out an "over-the-top" chocolate cake for the occasion. My father was always in "seventh heaven," with a smile from ear to ear! But, as my mother would always characteristically say "…why do we need a special day to tell one another that we love them? We say it every day of every year – I Love You!" And we did!

All our messages of Love would be displayed on the kitchen table for a week, then taken down and preserved by my mother – somewhere!

AND YOUR LOVE

And your love illuminates my life –
For longer than always.
All my love on Valentine's Day
Mitzi
February, 1963

HAPPY VALENTINE'S DAY

Weather forecast:

Skies of blue, with a rainbow or two

With Love's temperatures rising.

Remember me

Always!

Mitzi

February, 1967

ALWAYS IN LOVE

Happy Valentine!
To a wonderful couple
US!
Always in Love.
Love and Kisses,
Mitzi
February, 2003

…I LOVE YOU…

…More than you could ever know
I Love You!
Your devoted husband,
David
February, 2004

Inseparable and Still in Love!

MOVING DAY — MARCH, 1971

MOVING DAY – MARCH, 1971

March 23, 1971 – snowing! That date changed our lives forever, for it was on that day that we moved to PARADISE! Paradise was to be found in Brookville, Long Island on three acres. Our new home had been the original barn, carriage house and stables to the famed J.W. Woodward Estate. It had since been renovated after the sale and break-up of the original estate itself, and became our magnificent "new" home, which represented to my parents all their dreams having come true!

The morning of our move, excitement reigned! I was put in charge of rounding up all eight cats and putting them safely in my car for the trip to their new place of residence. The ride out to Brookville was characterized by a mix of howling and meowing. When I arrived, I had to oh – so – carefully take each cat and place them into our Cabana House where they would be safe, since the big front barn doors of our new home, would be open all day with the movers bringing in our precious "cargo." After I somehow managed to "unpack" each cat, I returned to our home in Great Neck, to witness its dismantling. It was controlled chaos with my mother and father directing! However, the end result would be life-changing! When everything finally reached its end, it was about 6:00 pm. Joyous, but exhausted, we were all smiles, with a sense of supreme satisfaction at our accomplishment, surrounded now, by our new home in Brookville, Long Island! However, "starving," we needed nourishment – dinner. I was elected, and drove to the nearest delicatessen, purchasing much of this and much of that, returning home with an over-abundance of delicious choices of precious food, for my parents and myself. We then all sat down in our new kitchen, to a well-deserved banquet, for our appetites were voracious, never having had stopped to eat since breakfast – including the cats! Well-fed and comfortably sated, we cleaned up our new kitchen, and went to sleep in our magnificent new home at our glorious new address!

This, our new life, actually began when my parents' Real Estate Agent located, after much searching, an "enchanted" Carriage House, with its lush gardens and pool. I can still vividly remember the excitement that ensued in our then home in Great Neck, when the Agent called to tell my parents of his find – it was electric! The idea of a Carriage House was tremendous, and after their initial visit, my parents were transformed, since it was this property and all of its structures, that created within themselves, a sense of euphoria, so strong and so definite, that it produced long remembered emotions and feelings reminiscent of their honeymoon at The Weirs in "their" cottage on Lake Winnipesaukee in New Hampshire. Now, this was their fairytale all over again! A torrent of memories overcame both my parents, for they walked onto this property and into this house, unknowing, when without warning, those oft dreamt of sentiments from that one fabled week came rushing back – and in disbelief, realized those feelings were brought back to the surface, by this property. My parents KNEW that this home represented "their" cottage, and that the grounds were representative of THOSE woods. They understood more than ever, that by acquiring this house and its surrounding gardens, that they would be reliving that fabled Honeymoon every day of their lives.

And so, I was sent by myself to see this house. My parents just said "…we want you to see it and then give us your opinion." That is all they had to say, for I jumped at the opportunity! Thrilled, I got all dressed up, and drove out to Brookville on this exciting "assignment." When I arrived, I could not get over the driveway! It was tremendous, and the garage was just as spectacular, for it had been the original stables, and now it housed cars! Immediately, I was in awe and beginning to become aware of how extraordinary this day was going to be. When I got out of my car and rang the bell, all I could focus on was the thought that I had never encountered a home as magnificent as this. It was right out of "Storyland." The present owners had been expecting me and gave me a big welcome when they opened the door, and thus commenced the "grand tour." I actually became somewhat hypnotized, for I had never seen anything quite like this, and kept repeating how "elegant and gorgeous" it was, without trying to seem too excited! I never imagined that a home as grand as this, could be found in this world! Then when I saw what would become my room and living quarters, I almost fainted! At a total loss for words, I was unable for once, to properly define my feelings and reactions. Afterwards, the tour graduated to the outside gardens, pool, cabana, bridle paths, and magnificent old flower pots. I was SOLD! Graciously, I thanked them and, in a "breathless" manner left for home to tell my parents that this had to be our new address!

On my drive back to Great Neck, my mind was spinning! I was plotting and planning on how to persuade my mother and father to buy this house that I believed I couldn't live without and would tell them that neither could they. Ultimately, when I arrived back from my expedition, my parents could not wait to speak with me and see my reaction, for they "KNEW." I walked into our kitchen and said "…You have to get that house! That is the only one for us!" My mother was laughing and ecstatic, and so too was my father! They then announced "…It's ours!" They had already bought it, but told the present owners not to let on – my parents wanted to be the ones to tell me of the extraordinary news! Immediately I started screaming and jumping up and down. Everyone was hugging and kissing. However, they hadn't mentioned "The Weirs" to me – not yet.

Moving day was thrilling, and all the subsequent days, weeks, and years that we lived in what my mother called my parents' "Dream Home," were just as or even more so! My parents were never happier. It actually was a fairytale that had inexplicably come true! Eventually, my mother told me that this house and all its surroundings – three acres of sumptuous landscapes and lush gardens – was "love at first sight," for both she and my father, instantly reminding them of their fabled honeymoon cottage. They never forgot that honeymoon, and were now able to re-live it, here in Brookville, every day of their lives! From that moment on, they always spoke about the Weirs, always incorporating it, somehow, and that one magical week. Now they were able to replicate that feeling forevermore! Divine Intervention had occurred, presenting this home with its magical aura to my parents and myself.

And so, my mother being truly overcome with emotion that my father bought this, their "honeymoon cottage," that she presented him with a card and her message of love.

DEAREST DAVID

Dearest David –
Thank you for everything –
Especially for your SELF
And all the glorious hours
Planned and unplanned.
The beach led to The Weirs
And the Weirs led to this –
The fulfillment of all our dreams
In our Dream House.
All my love ALWAYS
Mitzi
March, 1971

MOTHER'S DAY

Pauli and Mitzi, 1965

MOTHER'S DAY

Mother's Day! I was always very excited when this momentous occasion arrived – I think even more so than my mother. Habitually "chomping at the bit," I couldn't wait to present her with my cards that I put so much time and effort into selecting – I truly put all my love and kisses into this endeavor, that would begin weeks before the actual day. When weekends would "roll around," I would go from boutique to boutique searching for glorious cards, never being able to make up my mind, and so, rather than agonizing over choices, I always ended up purchasing three – my magical number!

The evening before the "big" day, I would unfailingly place my heartfelt cards on the kitchen table – carefully – so my mother would be sure to find them in the morning, as she was always the first to arise. However, they would also be surrounded by my father's cards, for he too, would place his "messages of love" with the greatest of care, in what he believed to be "his" strategic spot, once again, always having two or three cards himself. My father invariably wanted to make sure that my mother knew HOW much HE loved HER! And so, in order to make this purchase of major importance, my father travelled to his cache of secretive haunts – he NEVER gave them up, always smiling and smirking when asked, never ever revealing this most confidential of information! When the all-important day arrived, the three of us would gather around our famous kitchen table and read these wonderful cards, asking everyone "…where did you ever find them?" No one ever told! Smiling, my mother thanked us both, with a big hug and a big kiss for each! Then, my father would go off to our club to play his round of golf with his "cronies." Subsequently, my mother and I would immediately take advantage of our leisure time, going out to the backyard for a quick swim in our beloved pool, coming back in, and getting all "dolled-up," then driving to the club to have our Mother's Day luncheon celebration! My mother and I would unfailingly order a lunch that was never less than "divine!" Then, after my father's game of golf had come to an end, he would inevitably rush to take his place at our table, order his lunch, and join in the chatter about the day's events. A seven-layer cake would "surprisingly" arrive for dessert, which we somehow devoured – my mother had "secretly" called the Grill Room, to place her very special request with the Pastry Chef, and he complied! After we were fully sated, we hurried home to our backyard and pool, where we delighted in an afternoon of fun, frolic and music – always with Placido Domingo wafting through the air. To end the day, my mother served us her sensational ice cream sodas, putting twinkles in my father's eyes!

However, there happened to be one very different Mother's Day of which I have vivid memories! It was the year 1960, when I was ten and a half years old, and I was about to present my mother and my father with a Mother's Day gift that would be extraordinary, to say the least! Both would never forget that day when I came home and bestowed them with my "special" gift. MEASLES! My parents were aghast! And I was simply miserable. My father could not remember if he had had them, and so he was told by the doctor not to come near me for one week. My mother thankfully, had remembered having them when she was a child, therefore, she was able to care for me. However, I was told by my Doctor, that I had to stay in a darkened room for one whole week. No television, and no light – but it didn't matter, since I slept for practically the entire time. Then, slowly and "miraculously," I got better, and began to ever so slowly feel like myself. What was exciting, was that I was out of school for two weeks, and upon my return, was treated as if I had attained celebrity status! Everyone wanted to "hear" about my "ordeal!" However, to make my recovery "exciting" rather than "dull," my mother became quite inventive, sitting with me in my room composing little poems and stories, for which I always put in my "two cents!" I remember one of those poems to be "MEASLES," of all things! It was brilliant, and we read it over and over again, laughing and having so much fun. When I was able, I typed it up, and presented it to her as my "official" Mother's Day greeting! Now, I am of the realization that she purposely saved that precious poem all these years, for how could she have ever discarded something so "special," not to forget, priceless? Somehow, it has now magically resurfaced, just in time for another Mother's Day!

MEASLES

When you get the measles

You always get the sneezles.

You have to lie in bed all day

And cannot even go out to play!

All you can do is look up at the ceiling

And in your head there is an awful feeling!

Pills by the dozen you must take

And all kinds of medicine to relieve the ache!

The afternoon drags and seems so long

And with the whole day there is always something wrong!

By Pauli Rose Libsohn, May 1960, when I had the measles!

(Edited by Mitzi Libsohn)

FATHER'S DAY

Pauli and David, 1997

FATHER'S DAY

Our Father's Day celebrations inimitably took place on the Saturday before the "big" day, since my mother would, without fail, buy my father a new outfit to wear for golf at our beloved country club, and wanted him to make his "grand appearance," the morning of Father's Day itself. Therefore, that Saturday, my mother would "corral" my father when he arrived home after an exciting day on the course, immediately sweeping him into the kitchen to open his gifts – always a new and colorful golf shirt – orange, turquoise, raspberry, peach, gold – with a pair of shorts and pants to match. Protesting all the way, my father was outnumbered and always gave in! He really loved his new outfits and couldn't wait to wear them at the club to show-off! In my mother's eyes, my father always had to be perfect – she made sure of that!

On the actual day itself, my mother and I would present my father with his "fabulous" cards, of which there were several. This ceremonious affair occurred when we were all out at our pool, when my father came home from golf. My mother would then say "…did anyone comment on your outfit?" My father would answer "…what do they know?" followed by "…yes, one or two of the fellows said 'boy what an outfit, our wives don't get us clothes like that!'" Then my father, grinning all the while, said he replied with "…you don't have my wife, she's terrific!" He would then say to my mother "…you're the greatest lovey!" and give her a great big kiss! After changing into his bathing suit, he would come out to the pool to be with my mother and myself, with my mother having prepared her "famous" ice cream sodas, waiting for the "guest of honor" to arrive. When my father sat down, I assisted my mother in serving these over-the-top sodas to us all, with my father saying over and over "ooooooh boy, Mit, this is the greatest – you are something!" And our celebration began! There was laughter, swimming and splashing in the pool, music from Placido Domingo playing from the cabana, and of course picture taking! A fun time was definitely had by all, especially my father!!!

That evening we would continue the celebration with a big strawberry shortcake, which was one of my father's favorites, ordered and purchased at an exclusive French bakery. But before "digging in," my mother served in his honor, one of my father's favorite meals for our dinner, with the table also being decorated with all our cards, so that throughout the evening, we could read and re-read them. Then, those very cards, would all stay in place on the kitchen table for one week's time. My father was in heaven!

However, there was one Father's Day that was different from all others – that reason being due to my mother and her creative spirit. Unbeknownst to either myself or my father, she had made a secretive and extraordinary purchase – one in which she actually stepped out of character. Very quietly, and "on the sly," my mother had special ordered the CD, "Fats Domino's Greatest Hits," for she had somehow "fallen in love" with the song "Shake, Rattle and Roll." Therefore, the only way in which she believed she could present us with this new "love" was to gift it to my father for Father's Day. And so, when that particular day arrived, it began as any other with its normal celebrations. But, when my father came home from golfing, my mother excitedly led him out to our back patio at our pool, with myself in hot pursuit! With a smug look on her face, she proceeded to sit him down. She then turned and went into the cabana, coming out with a small gift, wrapped in beautiful tissue. "Open it!" she instructed, as she presented it to him. Happily, my father followed her directive, and as the tissue paper came off, the look that came over my father's face was priceless, with him saying "…what's this?" as roars of laugher came from both him and my mother! I, myself screamed "…what?" And as my father, my mother, and I, roared with that laughter, my mother somehow managed to have me put the CD into our stereo player, proceeding to play her "favorite," Fats Domino. My father not knowing what to make of this, followed the lead of my mother, as did I. And the strains of our laughter that ensued, were non-stop! My parents were hysterical, and my mother, determined, pulled my father up out of his chair, with the two of them still laughing and carrying on, as they took one another into their arms and began to dance their own version of the Lindy Hop.

It was truly unbelievable – what an incredible time they were having. And when the song "Shake, Rattle, and Roll" finally did come on, my mother and my father actually improvised and sang along, producing once again, waves of non-stop laughter. Not being able to withstand all this, they collapsed hysterically into one another's arms. It was from that day on, that the two of them would on occasion, play the Fats Domino CD, eventually fast forwarding to his signature "Shake, Rattle, and Roll," singing and dancing up a storm on our back patio! That Father's Day has never left my memory – it was truly unique! I'm sure my father never forgot it either.

In addition to all this, I remember one very special Father's Day celebration, due to another gift that my mother had also secretly purchased. It happened that one of my mother's favorite hobbies and pastimes was antiquing. She had her special and best-loved haunts that she was forever frequenting. One day, she happened upon a beautiful old and very large coffee cup – porcelain, I believe. Her excitement over this rare find was tremendous, and bought it immediately. Upon her return home, she was quite animated and thrilled about this purchase, calling me into the kitchen to immediately take a look! My initial thought was that it was certainly very old and worn, looking well-used. However, I noticed the beautiful and rare gold filigree around its rim and bottom, while in the center of this precious cup, in large gold calligraphy, was the word FATHER! It was then that I caught my breath, and had the same sense of excitement and thrill that my mother possessed. Now I realized why my mother was sooo elated – it was perfect for my father, for he would now have a cup all his own, for his after-dinner tea! Then, I watched as my mother took great pains and lovingly wrapped this rare, one-of-a-kind cup, in beautiful gold and white tissue paper, topped off with a big gold ribbon, to present it as a gift to my father on Father's Day. My mother planned the entire presentation, giving it to him at dinner, placing it in the middle of his dinner plate! I remember he said "…what's this?" He was gleaming, and started to laugh. Again, he said "…oh no, now what did you buy me?" He carefully tore it open, saying "…OH BOY!" His adoration of that cup was instant!

My mother was in heaven, and she bent over and gave him a great big kiss!

    My father drank his tea in that cup every night – that was HIS until the end. I have that mug today, tucked away in a drawer, safe and sound. HAPPY FATHER'S DAY.

LOVE TO THE BIG FISH...

Love to the big fish I swim around
With the best of all –
I'm baited, hooked, and caught
And want to stay on your line!
ALWAYS
Mitzi
June, 1965

Father's Day, 1968

HEY! HEY! GRADUATION DAY! 1967

HEY! HEY! GRADUATION DAY – 1967

The day of my highly heralded graduation from high school had finally arrived, after four long years of arduous and non-stop study! I myself could not believe that I was finally "getting out," graduating and going away to college! To commemorate this extraordinary event, my parents were taking me out to dinner at a fancy French restaurant – La Coquille, in Munsey Park, Long Island. This tremendous treat being given to me by my mother and father, had been planned for quite a while, and I was ecstatic, for when would I ever have the occasion to dine in such a "regal" atmosphere if not for my graduation – never! However, before the ceremony itself, my mother presented me with a gift that she agonized over, for she herself loved it, but wasn't sure about me. It was two giant Raggedy Ann and Raggedy Andy dolls! She presented it to me with such fanfare that my father and I realized that she actually used my graduation as an excuse to buy them for herself, for they were what SHE really wanted! My mother ADORED them. I tried to act as thrilled and surprised as possible when I was presented with this gift. However, my father saw my face, and said to my mother, "…what is she going to do with them?" "Never mind," was her reply, "I'm in charge." Pictures were taken with these gorgeous dolls, but my father and I wondered what WAS I actually going to do with them? My mother had ideas of her own! She bought an antique cradle, where she strategically placed both Raggedys – Ann and Andy, keeping this decorative acquisition on the second-floor landing of our home in Kensington in Great Neck. My mother adored those dolls, and they stayed with us until we moved from Brookville in 2005, selling them to an antique dealer who I believe adored them as much as she. Throughout the years, my mother always fussed with them, fixing their clothes, arranging them and propping them up. In Brookville, she placed them in that same cradle, only now they were on display in our spare bedroom, where they "lived" until we sold our home.

But my "real" graduation gift came in the form of a beloved Longines watch that I had wanted so very much. It was square shaped with a gold face and roman numerals. But what I loved the best was the brocade watch band. I thought that was the epitome of elegance! Persistently, and without let-up, I would bring my mother into our local jewelry store in Great Neck to admire it, and just pray that no one else would be swept away and buy it. But, unbeknownst to me, was that my parents had already purchased it, putting it away in a safe place, while the jeweler had ordered another which he had subsequently displayed in his cabinet of time pieces, and which I was always swooning over – the decoy! After my parents gave me my beloved watch, they told me how they had devised their plan! I was ecstatic! Yet the most meaningful part of this gift was the card that they wrote for me on this very special day of my achievement, being for me, quite moving and emotional. I then gave it a prominent "place of honor" in my room on my dresser, keeping it there for about one week, but after that I have no remembrance of what happened to that very precious card until today! Knowing my mother, she must have taken it and put it in a drawer in her dresser, saving it all these years, realizing its significance. It has now resurfaced after 41 years, looking just as new as when my parents presented it to me. That card was so filled with emotion, that my mother could not bear to part with it – she had an uncanny sense of its intrinsic value and she was right! Its discovery "blew me away," for it became a defining moment, forcing me to go into the recesses of my memory bank, with a new comprehension and full realization of the powerful emotion felt towards me by my parents. That card today, still has the same affect emotionally as it did all those years ago. My mother could never part with IT, and could never part with me! Not to be left out, nor could my father!

DEAREST PAULI

As you reach for the stars
Our love will always surround you.
Your beauty and creativity
Are a constant source of wonderment –
And delight.
May the lovely things in life always be yours!
But
Come to us for love and kisses.
From
Mommy and Daddy
Always!
June, 1967

DAVID'S BIRTHDAYS

David in his Birthday Hat at his desk, 2000

DAVID'S BIRTHDAYS

My father's birthday was in the summer in the month of July. It was always a ceremonious affair, with the biggest excitement being created over THE birthday cake! It was the most crucial and significant part of my father's "special" day – he LOVED Birthday Cake, especially HIS, with all the pomp and ceremony that surrounded it – the colorful candles all glowing when lit, the colorful party hats that my mother inevitably bought – us laughing and having such a good time – he never wanted that moment to end - he couldn't get enough! My mother and I always sang a rousing rendition of "Happy Birthday," which signaled my father to make a wish and blow out all his candles, usually on the first try. Then with a twinkle in his eye, he made the first cut in the cake, of which my mother always gave him a huge helping!

It was usual for my mother to begin to plan this all-important event some weeks in advance – lovingly designing the cake which would whet my father's palette and please his senses. Of course, she asked my advice, but what she decided upon, was ultimately the final decision. After "our" choice became definite, my mother would drive to her favorite bakery in Great Neck, Long Island, and place the order. She too was filled with anticipation and excitement over this first and foremost and most significant part of my father's celebration! However, the Saturday either before or after my father's actual birthday, would be the day on which we would all go out to dinner at my parent's country club to celebrate – inevitably telling the maitre'd about this momentous occasion! The evening would ultimately end with a special dessert being brought to the table with sparklers, ordered in advance by my mother, creating sparkles in my father's eyes! He was elated, secretly enjoying all the fuss and commotion being made just for him! And of course, the CAKE!

Always, for my father's "big" day, my mother would unfailingly bring out the "birthday hat" which she had found some years ago in one of her favorite "haunts." Upon seeing this perfect "creation," a red white and blue cardboard Top Hat, she knew it would be ideal for this very special occasion. My mother was the one to always place it on my father's head, followed by a big kiss! And without fail, the next thing I knew, my parents would be rolling with laughter, with myself joining in the fun! Pictures were taken with "the hat," with my mother "directing," and poses were made. After my father's birthday week had come to an end, (for we always celebrated for one week), my mother would once again take that hat, and carefully pack it away for the following year.

In addition to all this, there would be the exchange of gifts, which would invariably mean a book for my father purchased by my mother! Always, he would be excited, and after my father opened that special gift, my mother would be sure to give him a short synopsis, with my father being drawn in and "hooked." He couldn't wait to start reading! Then, it was my turn. I would present him with my gift of clothing – a pair of shorts, a shirt that matched, some pants, and maybe a tie! Of course, my mother had purchased them all, telling me when she brought them home, "…I got these things for you to give to Daddy. Put them away so he doesn't see them until his birthday." I knew she had taken great care in her choices, knowing exactly what he needed. After I presented him with these precious purchases, and after watching my father's facial expressions while opening his wondrous gifts, (smiling all the while), there came immediately thereafter, the "highlight of the evening," the fashion show – my mother and I wanting to see the results of all "our" efforts! We had so much fun watching my father model – laughing and offering all sorts of comments! A joyful time was had by all, especially by my father – he had a BALL!

Another important part of this celebration, was the presentation of our beloved birthday cards, which my mother and I always went searching for – we wanted only the "best" and of course, the most unusual, always composing original lyrical messages and extraordinary literary sayings! We then placed those cards on our kitchen table for one week, reading and re-reading them at mealtimes – showing them off to one another, oohing and aahing over the illustrations and messages of love, along with our individual creative greetings! My mother and I never disappointed my father in terms of celebration, with my mother topping it off with her famous ice cream sodas for us all! As far as my father was concerned NO ONE could top her in that department! And at the end of "HIS" day, he always went to sleep happy, surrounded by our love.

David Celebrating!

Celebrating!

DARLING!

Darling!
Happy Birthday – Happy Happy Birthday
I love you my wonderful adorable husband!
I love you and it will always be this way for us.
Your adoring wife
Mit -
Ever-adoring!
July, 1945

DAVID DEAR

My true-love hath my heart, and I have his,
…I hold his dear, and mine he cannot miss,
There never was a better bargain driven:
My true-love hath my heart, and I have his.
His heart in me keeps him and me in one,
My heart in him his thoughts and senses guides:
He loves my heart…
I cherish his because in me it hides:
My true love hath my heart, and I have his.
Mitzi
July, 1950

HAPPY BIRTHDAY

Volumes of LOVE
And a bushel of bookish kisses
To the one I love.
Mitzi
July, 2001

Birthday Fun!

Fooling around in one another's arms!

Mitzi and David poolside, celebrating!

MITZI'S BIRTHDAYS

Mitzi on her birthday!

MITZI'S BIRTHDAYS

September 18th always meant "heavenly" cheese cake topped with fresh strawberries – one of my mother's favorite and choicest of delights! It was her birthday, and my father made sure to call our club to place his order with the pastry chef for a 15" round strawberry cheese confection with additional strawberries to be placed on the sides. The chef was always so glad to help out my father, especially if he knew it was for my mother! When ready, my father would personally pick it up, checking to make sure it was "over-the-top with those special strawberries," secretly bringing it home, putting it safely away in the refrigerator in our cabana house, until dinner! On the evening of our celebration, my father would bring in the cake himself, setting it on the table to the joy of my mother! We then proceeded to sing a wonderful chorus of "Happy Birthday," which my mother adored, but no candles were allowed – they would "spoil" the cake! My mother always served my father and myself one generous slice for each. After that, she had her own plans for this "outrageous" testament to culinary expertise! Every year for my mother's birthday we followed a tradition – that this fabulous cake was to be my mother's breakfast for her one special week, and no one was allowed to touch! Every morning thereafter, she would ceremoniously make herself a pot of coffee, and sit down with that magnificent strawberry cheese cake at the kitchen table – she was in "seventh heaven!" And so, when my mother put our precious piece of cake in front of us that evening, my father and I were already salivating, dreaming, knowing we would have to remember the experience until next year! We devoured our precious serving, savoring each precious morsel. If, however, during the course of the week, she spied either one of us looking at that cake, she would laughingly say "…what are you doing?" We would break into laughter, sometimes having to sit down, guilt written all over our faces, and she would say, "…all right you can have a little piece – but just a little!"

In addition, my mother always had our club luncheon chef prepare one of her favorite meals for her Birthday Lunch, calling her order in to make sure they would start the preparations before her arrival – plate-size thin Blini, with sautéed apples, and gobs of fresh, cold sour cream on the side! It was fantastic – so much so that I ALWAYS left my place of business to join her, while my father delayed going to the office until after lunch – he too would not miss this meal! It was a delicious celebration, with chocolate cake and ice cream for dessert! It was divine in every sense of the word!

Another one of our forever traditions, was our beloved Birthday Cards, and my mother's birthday was no exception to the commotion that ensued because of them! My father had his secrets, and he unfailingly came up with the most gorgeous and original cards for my mother, and oh so quietly left them out on our kitchen table the night before this "grand" day, as were all three of mine! I too had gone on a search, looking for the "best" cards in the "world!" Habitually, my mother would be the first to enter the kitchen in the mornings, and we knew it, therefore we always made sure she would be greeted by our messages of love. When my father and I finally came in for our breakfasts, all our cards were displayed in a most artistic fashion, all on that famous kitchen table. Hugs and kisses were exchanged, along with the traditional "ooohs" and "aaahs." The cards stayed for a week, being admired and read over and over. It was grand!

And, let's not forget the books! My mother would consistently drop hints to my father and myself about what book and author she would love to have in our library. My father would always pick out a title he felt would engross my mother, always being "right on the money." He would then send me to Barnes and Noble to make the purchase, bringing it home unwrapped so he could inscribe it with much love, only then instructing me to "wrap it up!" That too, would be waiting on the kitchen table in the morning, amongst my mother's piles of cards. Always, her curiosity got the best of her, never disappointing, and ripped open the "secret" package, to see what her next read would be!

One special year, however, 1996, came to be one of the most extraordinary, for as my mother's birthday neared, she announced that she would like a new car – but not just any car, she wanted a NEW, 1976 Cadillac Eldorado Biarritz Convertible, white, with a white convertible top, and red leather interior, with a possible red pinstripe on the outside! That was some "tall" order – but that didn't scare my father – knowing that I work at an automobile dealership, he asked me to investigate to see if anyone had any connections – especially with a collector. At that time, however, my mother was already driving a Cadillac Eldorado Convertible – her all-time favorite car – and would drive no other, and my father knew it. Now, she felt it was time to get a new one, and would ONLY accept that model. Funnily enough, as luck would have it, one of the salesmen whom I decided to approach, had a friend who WAS a collector of automobiles. Excitedly I asked him to telephone them "right away," and apprise them of my mother's request. Divine Intervention occurred! That collector happened to be the RIGHT collector, since the salesman came back to me saying that they HAD one such car up on blocks in their garage, with 576 original miles! I was in complete disbelief, as was he! I actually almost lost my breath! In less than an instant I telephoned my father, who was astounded, for to locate a car such as this, just by asking a question and making ONE phone call, is unheard of! After all, it had no longer been in production for twenty years – thus the only explanation was, Divine Intervention! My mother kept saying over and over "…I just had a feeling I would find it – I just knew it." It her famous SIXTH SENSE! And so, I had the salesman arrange a meeting between the collector and my parents for the very next day. Both my mother and my father could not believe this "miracle," and on the following day went to meet them to see my mother's dream car! The atmosphere was electric. Then, I received that fateful telephone call – it was my father – they bought the car! It was gorgeous. My mother fell in love the moment her eyes saw this magnificent creation! It was love at first sight, and my father knew she was not going home without it. The collector could not believe their luck either, since they were moving and selling all their cars. They actually "needed" my mother, and when they saw that it was "true love," they were thrilled that someone like this was to be the recipient of their precious and rare automobile. The agreement was that they would have the car fully checked out and prepared for delivery in one week's time. Everyone shook hands and the deal was done! For the next week, it was as if my parents were celebrating a "second honeymoon," for the atmosphere in our home was none short of miraculous!

When the day of delivery arrived, my parents went once again to the home of the collector, and thanked them over and over for their good fortune. My mother drove the car home with the top down, and never ever looked back! It was hers – she adored it – becoming energized each time she opened the door, turned the key, and drove off! However, she did "allow" my father to drive – sometimes! Together, they went everywhere in that car – and the positive energy that emanated from that Eldorado, was infectious, lasting forever! That car came to signify my mother. Whenever anyone spotted it on the road, they knew she was in the driver's seat – EVERYONE knew that white Eldorado – thus, they knew my mother – for it was rare, and so was she! Happy Birthday!

Mitzi in her beloved "Birthday" Eldorado!

TO MY WIFE

Happy Birthday
To My Wife
A beautiful person
I will always be yours.
With all my Love,
David
September 18, 1993

HAPPY BIRTHDAY DEAREST

Happy Birthday dearest
Forever and forevermore
Happy Birthday.
With all my love,
David
September, 18, 2000

THERE'S ONLY ONE YOU!

What truer words
Can express my thoughts
For you.
Your ever- loving husband,
David
September, 2001

HAPPY BIRTHDAY

With all my love
To the most wonderful wife
I could ever had had.
David
September 18, 2001

All dressed up for a birthday lunch!

FOR THE LOVE OF PAULI

Pauli opening presents on her 4th birthday

FOR THE LOVE OF PAULI

I entered into this world as a "Princess," surrounded by love from my adoring parents, showering me with hugs and kisses my entire life. Always, my mother recounted with great emotion, that from the very first moment she saw me at the instant I was born – she fell in love. Both she and my father were totally hooked – while at the same time, the very first thought that entered her mind, was how lucky I would forever be, since I was born on Armistice Day (Veteran's Day), November 11th, and would unfailingly have a day off from school. She kept rethinking about that exceptional fact over and over, smiling, knowing how happy and thrilled I would be to learn of my good fortune, thinking I would be the envy of all the children, for after all, whoever gets a holiday from school on their birthday? That was the very first gift she so proudly gave me. She told that story continually, since it was a pure stroke of luck – or was it planned for by a higher power? And of course, she was right! Every year I celebrated my birthday with giggles, knowing I would have a cherished day off from school!

Because of the exceptional love that I received from my parents, my birthday celebrations were always sublimely magical! From my very first memories, my parents went to great lengths to plan my parties, with games – Pin the Tail on the Donkey – prizes for the children, party hats, and of course CAKE! Then it would ultimately come time to open my treasured presents, creating sounds of ooohs and aaahs loudly echoing throughout, as I held each gift up so everyone could see, with my mother and father reading each card aloud, and me, thanking each of my friends. It was a ceremony in and of itself. That was the part that I loved the best. However, the lighting of the candles on my beautifully decorated birthday cake, making a wish, blowing out the candles, eating and savoring every cherished forkful of that anticipated cake, was a definite runner-up.

Every year, without fail, until I entered college, my parents always had some sort of party and big celebration planned. My childhood friends were always present, with invitations being sent out, RSVP's arriving, birthday cake being ordered, refreshments bought, and again, games and some sort of unusual entertainment and fun arranged for by my parents. I truly believe that they enjoyed all the excitement and merriment as much, if not more than myself, and my friends! However, as I grew, instead of having these parties at our home, we inevitably had them at restaurants, to which my friends were always invited. Some were luncheons at Addie Valens Ice Cream Parlor in Great Neck, (my favorite!), where we had my eleventh birthday party. I remember how worried I was that my guests would not be able to make it because it had snowed that day. I was so upset and kept asking my parents "…what are we going to do…?" but nary-a-one cancelled – after all, it was at Addie Valens – and as always, my party was a success! As I grew older, my birthday "parties" were planned for dinner, only then, with a few select friends. The gifts and surprises bestowed on me by my parents were extraordinary, and always presented with much love. When I was in college, and for all the years thereafter, my parents and I ALWAYS went to dinner with just ourselves, for a big celebration! Again, gifts and cards were exchanged, and it was a lovely evening for all. My father especially could not wait to go, since it afforded him a big piece of cake!

One birthday in particular that I remember was when I was all of four years old. My parents had hired a professional photographer as a surprise, to take pictures of my party. However, when I saw him, I instantly decided I did not like him. Why, I do not know, and when at each instance that I saw he was attempting to take my picture, I either looked away, or did not smile. My mother kept having to "trick" me, by keeping me occupied so that I would not "snarl" at this very lovely man, who was trying so hard to do his job! Eventually, I calmed down and forgot about him, and became involved in the joy and happiness of the party itself!

Another grand celebration, was my "Sweet Sixteen." I had always dreamed of a resplendent party with a band from my high school – Great Neck South Senior High – with everyone who would be invited, having to bring a date! Upon asking my parents, they agreed, but put a limit as to how many "couples" I could have in attendance. I was over the top with excitement! Immediately I went to work on my guest list, inviting just my "closest" of friends! Everyone was adrenalized at the thought of my party, for it was going to be at Patricia Murphy's Candlelight Room, in Manhasset, Long Island! Elegant, is the word to describe that restaurant, with fountains, paneling, and floral arrangements that were awe-inspiring! The day of the party arrived, and I was both exhilarated and electrified with excitement! My mother loaned me her black and white floor length houndstooth full skirt to wear along with her orange turtleneck sweater! She also provided me with her silver jewelry for the evening! My hair was done and so was my makeup – I looked gorgeous! My date was coming all the way from New Jersey, being driven by his parents, who would also be my guests at my parents' table. No other adults would be allowed as per MY orders! Also, I gave strict instructions that no photographs were to be taken. I wish now, that my parents had overridden those instructions! My date arrived with his gift for ME of Chanel No. 5! I was speechless! Thrilled beyond belief, the party began, with the band playing all the latest "hits." Everyone danced up a storm, and then took a break, as we all sat down and had a fabulous dinner. Afterwards, we danced and partied until 12 midnight, when we all said our goodbyes, and thanked my parents for providing us all with such an exceptional and remarkable evening. It was the "TOPS!"

Throughout my life, as my birthday approached, I never forgot the "joie de vivre" experienced by my parents as they prepared for this "grand and momentous" day! There were always feelings of elation and exuberance on their part, to make sure I had wonderful birthday memories, no matter my age! They would start weeks in advance in their search for appropriate Birthday Cards to present me with. Both my mother and father put tremendous time and effort into this, in order to come up with the "GREATEST" card of all, sometimes travelling to certain "boutique" card stores out of the area, just to achieve this goal, not only presenting me with one card, but two, three, four cards each, composing small poems and words of love. When I opened them, it was ceremonious, to say the least, for they could not wait for my reaction.

Now, what they instilled in me will always be remembered – that that ONE day out of the entire year – your Birthday - belongs solely to YOU! Celebrate YOUR day to the fullest! Always taking their advice, I unfailingly dress in a bright, beautiful and glamorous "creation," stepping out for the day, feeling like I'm on "top of the world," and have the best time ever! Thank you M and D!

Pauli in her birthday finery!

NOVEMBER, 1983

Happy Birthday.
Love to my favorite girl – always!
Even in pigtails!
Non-stop love and kisses,
Always,
Mommy

NOVEMBER, 1985

Pauli
I'm not Clowning!
From the tips of your toes
To the top of your hair
Have a GREAT DAY!
Love and Kisses
Daddy-O
Have a very wonderful Birthday!

NOVEMBER 11, 1988

Pauli
Like a true work of ART,
You are many different things at once…
All precious to me!
LOVE,
Mommy

NOVEMBER 11, 1991

Dear Pauli –

You never cease to dazzle

All my love

To my beautiful

Rose

Mommy

NOVEMBER, 1996

Pauli

A special birthday Wish

To a special girl so precious to me!

My dearest and greatest joy!

All my love

Mommy

NOVEMBER, 1999

You did it!
Can you believe it?
A Happy Happy Birthday
With Millions of Kisses and Love
Daddy-O

NOVEMBER, 1999

Pauli
More candles mean more wishes –
May all your wishes come true.
All my love Always
To THE girl I love best in the whole world!
Love and Kisses,
Mommy

NOVEMBER, 1999

Pauli
Please be quiet
So that I can wish you
A very Happy Birthday!
Love and Kisses,
Your
Daddy-O

NOVEMBER 11, 2000

Pauli
You are truly gifted
And I'm all boxed in
Over you –
All my love,
Mommy

NOVEMBER 11, 2000

Pauli
Happy Birthday to my favorite person!
Are you smiling
Because
You're so
Fantastic?
Love and Kisses
From your favorite Daddy – O

NOVEMBER, 2000

Pauli
Vibrant
Original
That's you!
All my Love,
Mommy

NOVEMBER, 2001

Pauli

At three dollars a pound you are terrific!

The tomatoes at Youngs Farms are waiting for you!

Daddy-O

HAPPY BIRTHDAY

Pauli

Happy Birthday to

Our favorite Cupcake!

All our love

Mommy and Daddy

November, 2002

NOVEMBER, 2003

Pauli
Celebrate!
You deserve the Best!
Remember, no matter how many beautiful cupcakes
Your mother brings home to celebrate
None will be as GREAT as YOU!
Happy Birthday
Daddy – O

HAPPY BIRTHDAY

Happy Birthday

Pauli

Love to the most beautiful ROSE

In our garden.

You light up our lives!

Have a Brilliant Birthday!

Love

Mommy and Daddy

November, 2003

HAPPY BIRTHDAY!

Pauli.
We shower you with all our love –
And the best is yet to come!
Have an Epic birthday –
Wishing you joy and happiness always –
Hugs and Kisses
M and D
2003

DEAREST PAULI!

You are my favorite dish!

Happy Everything to someone Wonderful!

All my love

Always,

And Love and Kisses too!

Mommy

November, 2004

DEAREST PAULI!

Here is a golden flower

For a golden girl

On her golden day.

All my Love

Always,

Mommy

November, 2005

HAPPY BIRTHDAY — DEAREST PAULI

You are the most beautiful rose of all —

My happiness is you.

All my Love

Always,

Mommy

November, 2005

BIRTHDAY GIRL!

Hope your remarkable shoe collection

Takes you down the path

To the

Happiest Birthday

Ever!

Love

Mommy

November, 2007

NOVEMBER, 2007

Happy Birthday.
All my love to a darling daughter.
Beautiful and exciting always.
Always your "Mommy"
(Rain or Shine)

A THANK YOU FOR PAULI

A THANK YOU FOR PAULI

The beautiful message of love titled "Dear Pauli," which I uncovered as I sifted through all my family's old cards and letters saved by none other than my mother, has for me, special significance. I am ashamed to say however, that I cannot even remember receiving this card. Of it, I have no memory or recollection. Therefore, I was both floored and taken aback. So moved was I by this discovery, that I at once began to reflect on its meaning. The butterfly that my mother refers to, is representational of the gorgeous poem she penned, titled no less than "The Butterfly." That poem was one in her collection of almost two hundred which she composed, and was the reason why I was so adamant, and never gave up, in my quest to assure both her and my father, that my mother's writings were "written gold," easily equaling that of a professional like the American Poet, Robert Frost – for it was his collection of poetry which I purchased all those years ago, that proved to me that my mother's poems were made up of "poetic jewels." With that one thought in mind, I eventually, successfully and unconditionally, convinced my mother and of course my father, that we should work on creating a manuscript from my mother's poetic endeavors. That belief never left me – I believed in my mother, and from that moment on was responsible for the big push behind creating and producing her manuscript, which was to be the start of our journey into the unknown.

    I became driven and committed to this grand effort, focused only on producing a magnificent manuscript for her and the possible publishers that I was determined to "capture," wanting both my mother and my father to realize what I had known – that these poems were brilliant romantic verse. And so, my mother "got to work," and came up with a title for her manuscript and prospective book – "Confessions Of a Poet." Now, she was in rhythm, and was as excited about this project as was I. Creating this manuscript took months of hard work between the two of us, with my father poking his head in for "good luck." At its completion I ceremoniously presented the finished and final "product" to my unsuspecting parents one evening after we had finished our dinner, saying to them in a most nonchalant manner, "…do you have a minute?" Not knowing what to expect, they replied "…of course we do for you – anything!" I then left the kitchen, and returned to ceremoniously present them with the finished "creation!" They were in awe and unbelieving at what I had brought forth! My mother was speechless, and my father said "…I always knew you had it in you!" There were hugs and kisses, and disbelief! My parents could not believe what I had done, and it was all because of my homework assignment in my creative writing class, to write a poem, that gave my mother the idea to write one herself, producing an avalanche of poetry, that ceaselessly flowed from her pen and onto her yellow-lined pad! Never once, did I ever give up on her creative ability and brilliance, now bringing it to fruition! My parents were floating on air, and I immediately stated, "…we will now find a publisher!" The rest is history – SIX BOOKS – and still sharing her writings with the world!

DEAR PAULI

Here is 'The Butterfly"
That flew out of the manuscript
You so brilliantly composed.
Please cherish it as we cherish you!
All our love always –
M and D
November, 2002

A DAUGHTER'S NOTE

This creative work, compiled solely of my parents' original verses of poetry and letters of love, is an artistic effort relating to and involving their lives throughout the years, in essence, telling their story. Their passion "unleashed" their creative energy and can be observed in these "messages of love," composed for all and various occasions, written on gorgeous greeting cards purchased, with that very love, which they believed warranted these, their intimate communiques, belonging solely to them.

No one that I am aware of today, communicates with such cards and letters – those of decades gone by, as did my parents. They spoke the language of love through the written word and thrilled to the sight of a card or letter, for they knew they would be the recipient of those precious "messages of love."

With this original compilation, I believe I have brought insight into how generations before, "spoke" in this uniquely non-verbal style of passion, exchanging words in beautiful penmanship, putting it all down on gorgeous cards and paper. The art of love's expression, is practically non-existent in today's world. Lovers of years gone by, have been lost to the ages, but with this discovered work, I am able to show, the true meaning of Love's written word.

I can now genuinely say for sure, that I have fully completed my promise to my mother and my father. All their literary endeavors have been discovered, found, edited and published by me, their devoted daughter, with the greatest of love. There is nothing left to uncover – I have completed my search, which has culminated in two published volumes of my mother's poetry – "Immortal Kisses – Confessions Of a Poet," and "Songs Of You – A Postscript," one book of her essays – "Silhouettes – Literary Passageways," an edition of her papers on her beloved Shakespeare – "My Mother and Shakespeare – A Daughter's Journey," and now this, lost love letters, along with both my parents' greeting cards' messages of love. Ultimately, through these very books, I created a book of my own – MY loving biography, "What Is Love," and told my parents' story through my eyes and remembrances.

Thus, throughout this journey, I have learned about aspects of my parents' lives that I had NEVER known, achieving an understanding about them that I again, would NEVER have had, if it had not been for this project. It is with a certain sense of sadness that this has now come to its conclusion, yet I have tremendous feelings of reward and fulfillment, triumph and achievement, satisfaction and accomplishment. It was essential to me that I be able to keep my promise – however, it developed into something so big, that it was above and beyond any of my wildest dreams. I know my parents are dancing in Heaven!

Now, upon reaching the end of my parents' story, I can truly say, that a sense of incredible achievement as well as a supreme sense of pride has occurred within myself, due to my completion of this gorgeous and monumental anthology – I have immortalized the fairy tale that began with a book and a dream – a bond of love and passion that could never be broken and that will continue forever and ever more, all due to a promise kept.

Pauli Rose Libsohn

CPSIA information can be obtained
at www.ICGtesting.com
Printed in the USA
JSHW011638300520
5987JS00006B/17